About this book

This book was inspired by the works of a young person named Ethan Joseph. Ethan is autistic and uses art as a means of expression. His art has long taken the interests of adults and young people alike. Ethan has a natural ability to create beautiful and symmetrical drawings with little effort. While creating these works of art, Ethan works very quickly and seemingly without thought.

When posed with the idea of using his artwork to create a book, Ethan immediately suggested making an animal alphabet book. With this readiness, he produced the artworks for each letter of the alphabet. With the support of his teachers and the Black Gold Publishing team, this Animal Alphabet book was created to bring an element of fun to early learning.

We hope you and the young learners enjoy the journey through Ethan's Animal Alphabet.

Contributions from
Ethan Joseph

Written & Edited by
Miguel Alexander
Nikhita Jaya

Aa

The armadillo can roll into a ball.

Armadillo

Bb The buzzard can fly over 1000 metres high.

Buzzard

Cc
The coyote can make 11 different types of sound.

Coyote

Dd There are over 200 different breeds of dogs.

Dog

PRACTICE WRITING
ANIMAL NAMES

A

Armadillo
Armadillo
Armadillo
Armadillo
Armadillo

B

Buzzard
Buzzard
Buzzard
Buzzard
Buzzard

C

Coyote
Coyote
Coyote
Coyote
Coyote

D

Dog Dog
Dog Dog
Dog Dog
Dog Dog
Dog Dog

Ee

The oldest known elephant in the world lived for 86 years.

Elephant

Ff

Fish can breathe under water.

Fish

Gg

A giraffe is theworld's tallest land animal.

Giraffe

Hh Hippos mostly eat grass.

Hippo

CREATE A SCENE WITH THE ANIMALS

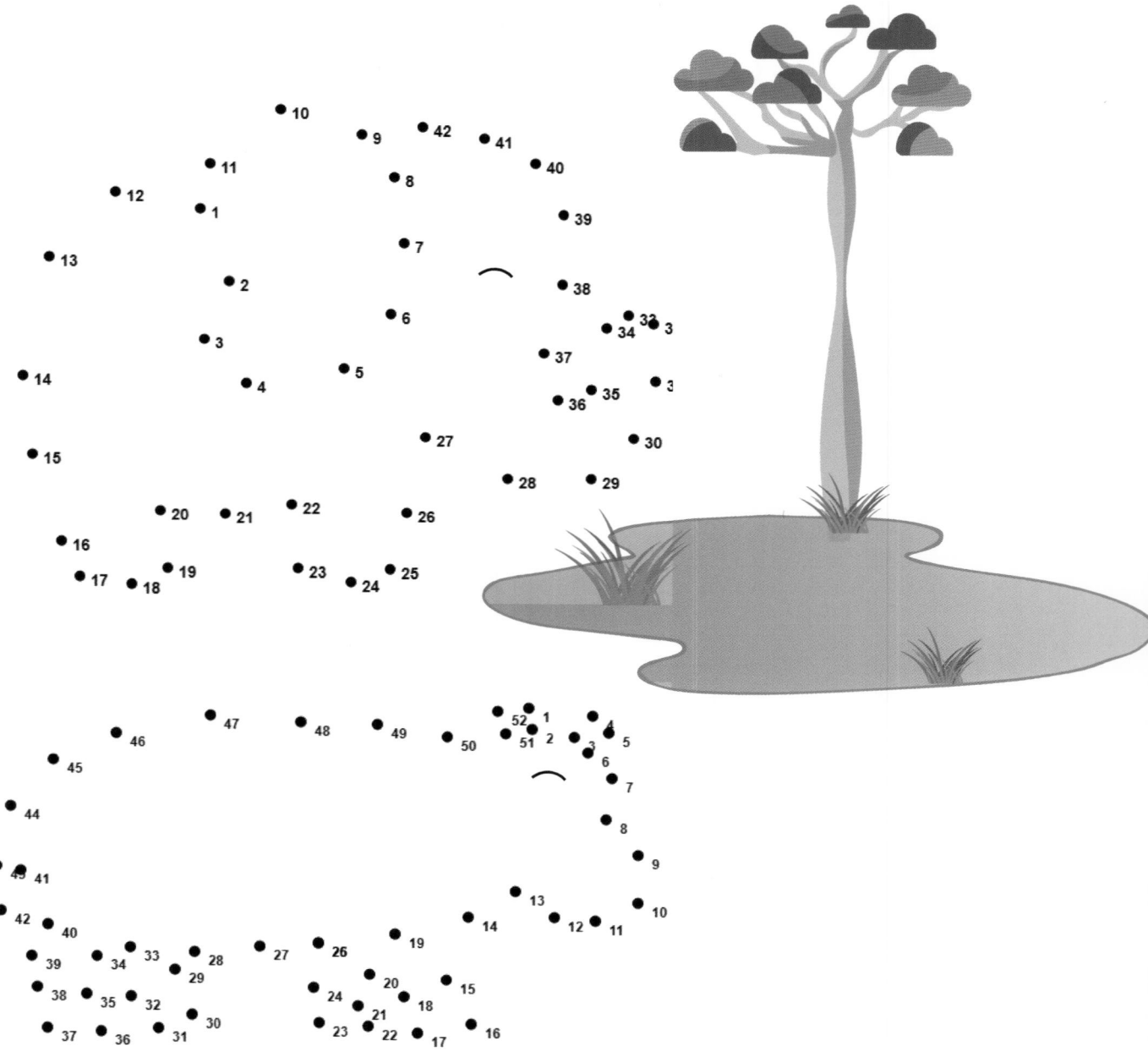

Ii Iguanas are the largest lizards in the Americas.

Iguana

Jj

Jaguars are the third largest cat in the world.

Kk A new born koala is called a joey.

Koala

Ll

A lion has a very loud roar.

Lion

WHICH IS THE ODD ONE OUT?

Mm

A mouse can eat up to 20 times a day.

Mouse

Nn

A narwhal is a type of whale with a tusk.

Narwhal

Oo

An octopus can change into many colours.

Octopus

P p Penguins are birds that cannot fly.

Penguin

MATCH THE ANIMALS TO THEIR HOMES

Qq

Quails nest on the ground.

Quail

Rr Rabbits have an excellent sense of smell.

Rabbit

Ss Snakes can smell with their tongues.

Snake

Tt Tigers seem to enjoy water and swim well.

Tiger

ANINAMES
UNSCRAMBLE THE WORDS AND MATCH THEM TO THE CORRECT ANIMAL

_____ _____ _____

_____ _____ _____

tabirb   laqiu   kya
egrit   keans   guennip

Uu Umbrella birds come from central and southern America.

Umbrella Bird

Vv Vultures are found everywhere in the world, except for Australia and Antarctica.

Vulture

Ww

The blue whale is the largest mammal in the world.

Whale

ANIMART
COMPLETE THE ANIMAL DRAWINGS

Xx

Xeme is a small gull that lives in the artic.

Yy Yaks live in high places in the world.

Yak

Zz A group of zebras is called a dazzle.

Zebra

ALPHABET

PRACTICE YOUR
WRITING SKILLS

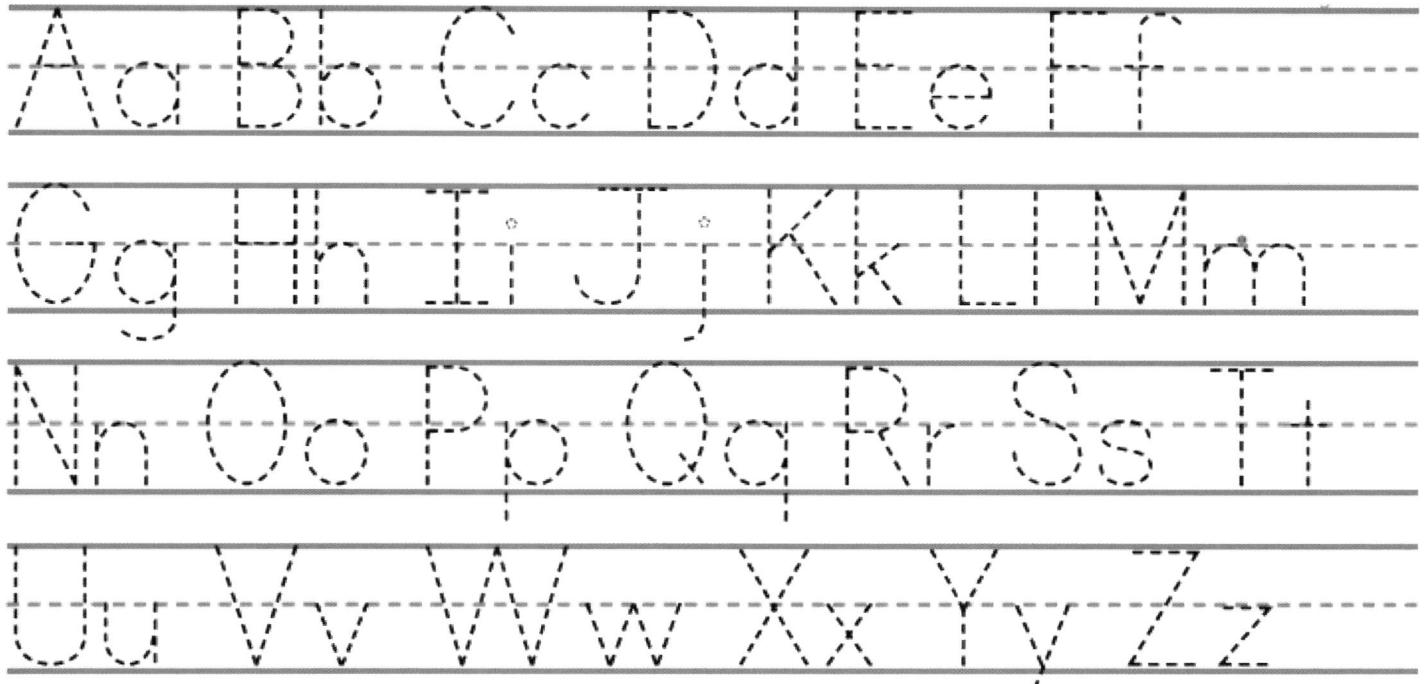

.... AND NOW I
KNOW MY ABC.

PINGU

Goes to Playgroup

BBC CHILDREN'S BOOKS

Pinga was cross. Everyone seemed to have forgotten that she was going to playgroup today.

"Hurry up!" she kept shouting as she stood ready by the door. "I want to go."

Mum was busy ironing.

"I want to go to playgroup NOW!" shouted Pinga.

"Oh, my goodness," said Mum, "I'd forgotten all about it. Pingu had better take you this morning."

Pingu was busy too. He was reading his favourite comic.

"Pingu!" yelled Pinga. "I want to go to playgroup. Mum says you've got to take me NOW."

"All right, all right," said Pingu.

On their way to playgroup Pingu and Pinga saw two friends tobogganing down a steep slope. It looked fun.

"Hey, Pingu!" they called out. "Come and play with us."

"I can't," explained Pingu. "I'm going to playgroup."

The two friends laughed. "He's a bit old for playgroup, isn't he?" they said to one another.

Playgroup had already started by the time Pingu and Pinga arrived.

"I'm sorry we're late," said Pinga in a nervous, squeaky voice.

"That's all right, little Pinga," said the teacher, smiling.

"And you must be Pinga's brother," said the teacher, greeting Pingu. "Perhaps you'd like to join in the fun this morning."

"I think I'm a bit old for playgroup," said Pingu.

As Pinga made her way over to her seat she suddenly slipped up and fell flat on her face. Pingu rushed over to help her up.

"Are you all right?" he said, anxiously.

"Today we are going to do some paper folding," said the teacher. "I shall show you how to make a paper hat. Just copy me."

All the little penguins set to work, except for Pinga.

"Come on, Pinga. That looks fun," said Pingu.

"I can't do it," said Pinga in a worried voice.

"Don't worry. I'll help you," said Pingu. He went up to the teacher to ask for some paper of his own.

"Perhaps I will stay after all," he said to the teacher.

Pingu folded the paper quickly. First he made a hat for Pinga and then he made one for himself. He was beginning to enjoy himself!

The little penguins were very pleased with their hats.

"Look at me!" they all shouted to each other.

"Now we're going to do some dancing," said the teacher. She put a record on the gramophone and Pingu wound it up.

The little penguins all clapped their hands and marched along in time to the music. Pingu joined in too and had a wonderful time.

After the dancing, it was playtime. Pingu had a go on the slide first. He zoomed down it head first and went shooting off the end.

"Ha, ha!" laughed Pinga who was sitting at the top of the slide with a friend.

Pingu had only just stood up when Pinga and her friend came hurtling down the slide and knocked him over again.

"Thanks a lot!" said Pingu crossly.

Now it was story time. The little penguins sat quietly in a row while the teacher read them an exciting tale all about a snowman. Pingu enjoyed it just as much as everyone else.

And then it was time to go home.
"You've all been very good this morning,"
the teacher said as she waved her class goodbye.
"See you tomorrow."

"Goodbye, Pinga," said the teacher. "I hope you
liked having your brother at playgroup this morning."
"Oh, yes," said Pinga, "but he's a bit too big for it
really."

"Thank you," said Pingu to the teacher as he left.
"Playgroup is a lot of fun! Can I come again another
morning?"

"You can join us whenever you like," said the
teacher.

On their way home, Pingu and Pinga met their two friends again. The two penguins burst out laughing when they saw Pingu's hat.

"Hey, Pingu!" they shouted out. "We like the hat! Just right for playgroup."

23

Pingu was furious that they were making fun of him. "I'll show them what I can do with this hat," he said to himself.

Very quickly he refolded the paper hat into a boat and floated it on the nearby pond.

24

The friends laughed again.

"That boat's rubbish. It won't go very far," they jeered. They began to pelt it with snowballs from across the water.

"Hey!" shouted Pingu and Pinga together. "Stop that or you'll sink it."

"That's just what we want to do," the two friends shouted back. But the strange thing was that no matter how hard they tried to hit it, the boat kept dodging out of the way. They couldn't understand it at all.

Just then, the boat began to rise out of the water and who should appear under it but Pingu's best friend, Robby the seal! He grinned at everyone, looking very pleased with himself.

Pingu and Pinga jumped up and down with excitement.

"Robby!" they cried. "It was you all along!"

Robby barked with pleasure and began to do some acrobatics in the water, balancing the boat first on his nose and then on his tail.

Everyone clapped and cheered – even Pingu's two friends enjoyed the show.

Hurray for Robby the seal!

Published by BBC Children's Books
a division of BBC Worldwide Limited
Woodlands, 80 Wood Lane, London W12 0TT
First published 1996
Text and design copyright © 1996 BBC Children's Books
Stills copyright © 1996 Editoy/SRG/BBC Worldwide
Pingu copyright © 1996 Editoy/SRG/BBC Worldwide

ISBN 0 563 40443 4

Typeset by BBC Children's Books
Colour separations by DOT Gradations, Chelmsford
Printed and bound by Cambus Litho, East Kilbride